History in Col

Wendy Clemson

Stanley Thornes (Publishers) Ltd

Acknowledgements

Many children and their teachers from the following schools in Chester provided work for the photographs:
Boughton Heath CP School
Overleigh St Mary's CE Primary School
St Thomas of Canterbury CE Aided Junior School

My husband, David, helped behind the camera, and Frances, our daughter, offered much practical support and good humour. Some of the objects in the photographs will be very familiar to other members of the family, from whom they were borrowed.

I am indebted to Ron Adams, who has provided some stunning display photographs, which make the book more attractive and useful.

To all these people, and to Roger Crowley, Primary School Publisher, who saw the timeline for this book stretch ever longer, I wish to say thank you.

Text © Wendy Clemson 1999
Original line illustrations © Aetos Ltd. 1999
Original photographs on pages 1, 36, 40, 42, 44, 54, 58, 63, 64, 69, 71, 74, 75 and cover ©
Ron Adams 1999
Original photographs on all other pages © Wendy Clemson and David Clemson 1999

First published in 1999 by:
Stanley Thornes (Publishers) Ltd
Ellenborough House
Wellington Street
CHELTENHAM GL50 1YW
England

99 00 01 02 03/ 10 9 8 7 6 5 4 3 2 1

A catalogue record for this book is available from the British Library.
ISBN 0-7487-2951-8

Typeset by Aetos Ltd. Bathampton, Bath.
Printed in Hong Kong by Wing King Tong.

Contents

Section One

Section Two

Introduction

History in Colour is a book of creative ideas to enliven your teaching of history in the primary curriculum. It provides a vast collection of practical activities for the children to do. In addition to two-dimensional work - drawing and painting using an array of media - there are ideas for work that is three-dimensional.

The book is set out in double-page 'spreads'. Each spread addresses a different history topic. The spreads in the first section of the book are given general titles. Teachers working with classes at Key Stage 1 can either use these historical topics titles, or they can use the topics as part of more all-embracing work in the humanities or in other parts of the curriculum. Spreads in the second section tackle some aspects of the Key Stage 2 Study Units, which the children have to address in the National Curriculum. However, in providing ideas for art and craft work, both sections of the book should prove invaluable to all teachers.

In some instances the outcomes of the activities are shown as illustrations or in the photographs. But there are also photographs that stand alone and are additions to the activities described. Activities, illustrations and photographs are all intended to provide the inspiration for you to try out a range of media with the children in your class.

It is important that children begin to master the skills of the historian while they are still in primary school. Each spread lists some of the historical skills that can be worked on as the children do the activities. On the final spread of the book, there is a checklist of some of the experiences to which the children should have access in order to develop their skills in history.

Family

First activities

1 My family

Invite the children to say, in turn, who is in their immediate family (mum, dad, step-parents, foster parents, brothers, sisters). Tell the children what a 'portrait' is and ask them to draw or paint portraits of these people. Create a portrait gallery.

2 Grandparents

Ask the children about their grandparents. Check that the children know that these people are the parents of their parents, and that they are older (i.e. they have lived longer) than some of the other adults the children know. Invite the children to make 'photo-fit' pictures of their grandparents, using sticky shapes and yarn.

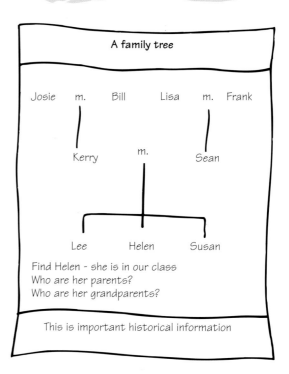

A family tree

Josie m. Bill   Lisa m. Frank

Kerry   m.   Sean

Lee   Helen   Susan

Find Helen - she is in our class
Who are her parents?
Who are her grandparents?

This is important historical information

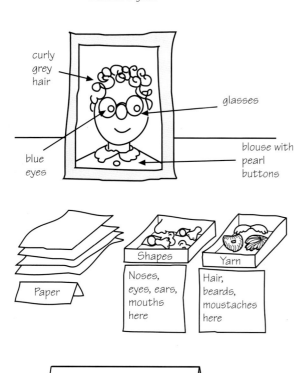

Gemma's gran

curly grey hair

glasses

blue eyes

blouse with pearl buttons

Paper

Shapes

Noses, eyes, ears, mouths here

Yarn

Hair, beards, moustaches here

Take what you need to make a picture of your granny or grandad

3 Family tree

Show the children how to draw out their own family tree of their grandparents, their parents and themselves. Point out that we each have four grandparents and two parents. Display the family trees to compare them, and talk about how the trees can be extended if we think back further into the past.

Resources

Poster paints and brushes; portrait-size paper; sticky paper; sugar paper; PVA glue; yarn

4 Family records

If any children have family records kept in a photograph album or the family bible, show these to the class. Point out that the family bible was often used as a record of the history of the family, and was passed on from parents to their children, and then to their children.

Further activities

1 Portraits from the past

Show the children some reproductions of paintings of people from the past. Allow the children to copy them, discussing clues in the pictures about the kinds of clothes people wore and the life they led. Point out that before photographs were invented, this was how wealthy people kept a permanent record.

2 Families in history

Take the children out of school to look for evidence of local families having a past. They can record shop signs and advertisements, e.g. 'Established in...', look for plaques showing where famous people may have lived, and view tombstones in a local churchyard.

Historical elements

chronology ✔
vocabulary of passing time ✔
experience the past as shown in
      pictures/writing/TV etc. ✔
using sources ✔
asking/answering questions ✔
communicating work ✔

3 Birthdate timeline

Draw a giant timeline that spans all the years of this century. Ask the children to supply information about birthdates in their families, which they can write on decorated cards. This information can then be attached to the line.

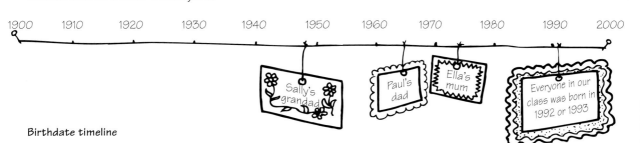

Birthdate timeline

Homes

First activities

1 Montage
Ask the children to cut out pictures of homes from magazines and newspapers. Make a large class montage so that the picture can be used as the basis of a class discussion about homes from different cultures and times.

2 My house
Encourage the children to draw or paint their own house and to find out how long ago it was built.

3 Our street
Invite the children to draw a picture of a building in the main street. An example of each building can be placed on a large class display. (The children can be taken along the street to look at the buildings, but they can use photographs back in the classroom to help them make their drawings.)

Resources
Magazines/newspapers with pictures of homes; sugar paper; crayons; felt-tipped pens; paints; modelling card and boxes; PVA glue; Artstraws

Historical elements
chronology ✓
vocabulary of passing time ✓
differences between times ✓
experience the past as shown in pictures/writing/TV etc. ✓
asking/answering questions ✓
communicating work ✓

Our main street
Which house is the oldest?
How do we know that a house is old?

My house by Am

Further activities

1 Heating

Help the children to find out how people heated their house in the past. A picture web display can be made with a fire at the centre, and pictures of open wood fires, open coal fires, gas fires, and central heating radiators drawn around it.

2 Lighting

The children can start with fire and candle flames as sources of light in people's homes. With adult help they can make a candle. Tell the children about the introduction of gas lighting, and the use of electric lights (only within the last 100 years or so).

3 Keeping clean

Help the children to find out how people kept clean in the past. Encourage the children to do drawings and make models of wringers and washing machines. Mount a class display.

9

Communication

First activities

1 Sending messages
Ask the children to help create a web of ideas showing the ways we use to get messages to one another. They can then draw pictures to illustrate the web. Talk to the children about ways of sending messages that date from thousands of years ago, and ways that are possible now because of modern technology.

2 Old writing instruments
Give the children opportunities to try writing with a range of instruments, including dip-in pens and slate pencils on slates. Old photographs of classrooms should show that slates were used by schoolchildren in Britain a century ago. The children can compare these instruments with the ball-point pens and pencils in use today.

3 The Post
Help the children to create a trail of the progress of a letter from the sender to its destination. Then tell the children about the history of the postal service. Allow them to look at and replicate old stamps and cards, and draw pictures of postmen and postwomen in uniforms of the past.

Resources
Card; sticky shapes; Cellophane; scissors; felt-tipped pens; long strips of paper for time trails; quill pens and dip-in pens; washable ink; good-quality writing paper; slates and slate pencils; computer with e-mail facility; gold and silver pens; coloured inks; potatoes; knife; sheet plastic; ink rollers; poster paints

Historical elements
vocabulary of passing time ✓
differences between times ✓
experience the past as shown in
    pictures/writing/TV etc. ✓
using sources ✓
asking/answering questions ✓
reasons and results ✓
communicating work ✓

The Post
A Penny Black stamp
A postman of long ago

Greetings
Thank you
These cards were sent long ago. There is a date on one of them. How long ago?
Hello!
How are you?
I miss you
1918
Happy Birthday

4 Electronic messages
Use computer software to e-mail children at another school and set up a regular correspondence about message sending now and in the past.

A quill pen

These seals are made from sealing wax

This is a modern copy of an old pen. This quill pen has a nib.

Here are the seals we made

Further activities

1 Before the Post

Examine in more detail some of the strategies people used in the past to send messages, including the carrying of 'sealed' messages by a messenger. (This can be compared with the motor cycle and van courier services today.) Show the children how letters were sealed and ask them to try using seals of their own, made from sealing wax or playdough.

2 Keeping a record

Explain to the children that if we wish to pass information on to other people, we not only send messages but keep records, produce newspapers, write books and make personal records such as diaries. Point out that diaries from the past tell us what life was like in other times. Show the children some 'official records' such as a birth certificate or the school log, and ask them to make an annotated record of a day in their own life.

3 A history of writing

Investigate the long history of peoples from the past making marks on parchment, papyrus and paper. Look at examples of the ways the letters in the alphabet have been written at different times. Show the children illuminated letters and ask them to make their own, using felt-tipped pens, gold and silver pens and coloured inks.

4 Getting into print

Tell the children about how 'print' is made and about Caxton and the invention of the printing press. The important point is that a block is made, inked and then pressed on to paper. The resulting image is a reversal of what is on the block. Allow the children to make prints of their own. They could try potato printing, or making monoprints.

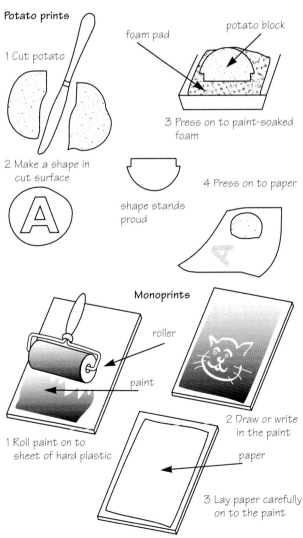

Potato prints

1 Cut potato

foam pad   potato block

3 Press on to paint-soaked foam

2 Make a shape in cut surface

A

shape stands proud

4 Press on to paper

Monoprints

roller

paint

1 Roll paint on to sheet of hard plastic

2 Draw or write in the paint

paper

3 Lay paper carefully on to the paint

11

Clothes

First activities

1 Why we wear clothes

Talk to the children about the reasons why people have worn clothes through the ages. Reasons may include: protection, custom (decency), decoration, and to show status. Look for pictures of people in different periods of history, and talk about and draw what they are wearing.

2 Pictures from the past

Ask the children to bring into school photographs that were taken in their own family many years ago. (Seek parents' permission, and ask parents to list the date of the photographs and who appears in them.) Look with the children at the clothes the people in the photographs are wearing. Ask the children to use charcoal or crayons to draw some of the images they see in the photographs. Display the children's work along with some special items of clothing, e.g. a Christening dress, first boot, or special hat.

Family photographs from the past

Can you see the buttons?

Look at the collar here

Our drawings

3 What is it made of?

Allow the children to handle and talk about some samples of different fabrics. Talk about the kinds of fabrics that were available in the past, and the use of special fabrics for the rich, for special occasions and for special people. The children can draw an outline of a person and then stick down fabric scraps to make suitable clothes.

4 Style

Show the children how to make card people who can be given costumes in a variety of styles.

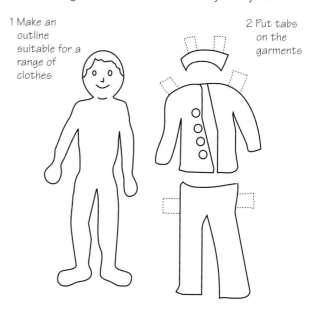

1 Make an outline suitable for a range of clothes

2 Put tabs on the garments

Historical elements

vocabulary of passing time ✔
differences between times ✔
experience the past as shown in pictures/writing/TV etc. ✔
using sources ✔
asking/answering questions ✔
communicating work ✔

Resources

Drawing paper; crayons; charcoal; scraps of different fabrics (e.g. wool, cotton, nylon, silk, satin, velvet, linen); large blunt needles; thick thread; Binka or similar fabric; a range of papers, brushes and paints

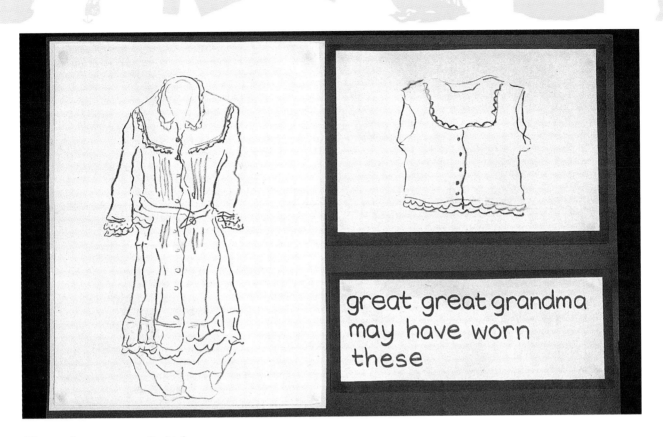

great great grandma may have worn these

Further activities

1 Armour

Make a special study of protective armour that soldiers have worn. Choose a soldier from the past and help the children create a life-sized, 3-D picture in card. Then make a class collage. Compare this outfit with a uniform worn by riot police today.

2 The making of clothes

Talk about how clothes are made. Discuss what the invention of the sewing machine has meant for the making of clothes. Examine an old sewing machine to see how it works. Using large blunt needles, thread and open work fabrics, allow the children to try out different sewing stitches.

3 Paintings from the past

Look at the clothes people are wearing in paintings, and at how the artists have created the look of folds, creases, and the surface texture of fabrics such as velvet and lace. Allow the children to experiment with different papers, brushes and paints to create texture effects.

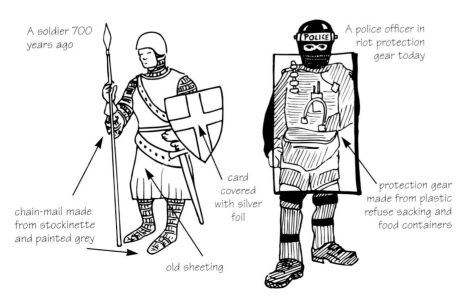

A soldier 700 years ago

A police officer in riot protection gear today

chain-mail made from stockinette and painted grey

old sheeting

card covered with silver foil

protection gear made from plastic refuse sacking and food containers

13

First activities

1 My toy
Ask the children about their own favourite toy, and invite them to paint or draw it.

2 Toys Mum and Dad had
Ask the children to talk to their parents about the toys they had. Compile a list of favourites. Search out pictures of these and ask the children to make direct comparisons between the toys their parents liked best and their own favourites. The comparison pictures can be displayed side by side and the children can write the display captions.

3 Toy theatre
Give the children the chance to make a cardboard theatre like those enjoyed by children in Britain around 90 or 100 years ago. The theatre can be modelled on a local one if there is a Victorian or Edwardian theatre in the town.

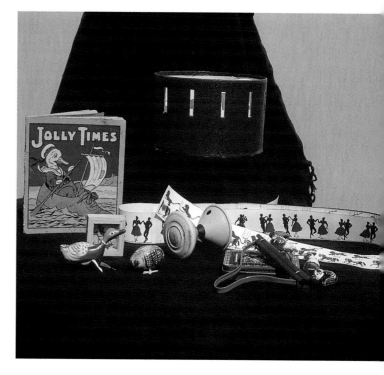

4 Toy museum
Set up a toy museum in the classroom with old toys, if available, and replica toys that the children have made. Soft toy teddies, peg dolls and models of carts and vans of the past could be included.

2 Cut around

4 Fold back here to make stage stand up

card outline

5 Cut out figures and attach to card strips

1 Cut from here around three sides

3 Fold back here to make stage

Further activities

1 Dolls' house

Collect shoeboxes so that the children can work alone or in pairs to make a room interior or a dolls' house in a period of their choosing. They will need access to a range of craft materials and PVA glue. Additional adult support with the research and construction would be invaluable.

2 Outdoor games

Invite the children to work in groups, exploring the history of an outdoor game. The children can find out when the game was first played, the rules and how they have changed, and the equipment and kit. They can draw and cut out outlines of equipment, showing how shapes have altered over the years.

Old tennis racquet   Modern tennis racquet

Historical elements

chronology ✓
vocabulary of passing time ✓
differences between times ✓
experience the past as shown in
    pictures/writing/TV etc. ✓
using sources ✓
asking/answering questions ✓
communicating work ✓

Resources

Paints and brushes; painting paper; card;
scissors; felt-tipped pens; wooden clothes
pegs; PVA glue; felt and other fabric
scraps; dowel or pea sticks; toy or
cushion filling; shoeboxes;
lace; sugar paper

Shoebox dolls' houses

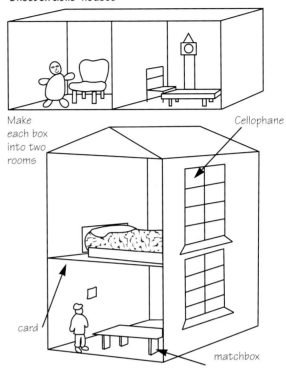

Make each box into two rooms

Cellophane

card

matchbox

Seaside holidays

First activities

1 Holiday souvenirs

Ask the children to bring in souvenirs and mementoes from holidays they have had. Talk about the idea of bringing home reminders of holidays. Explain that people in Britain were first able to take holidays in the last century. Seaside souvenirs such as items decorated with shells and coloured sands became popular then. Allow the children to draw old souvenirs, if available, or to make replicas. (Avoid using shells in the interests of environmental conservation.)

2 Treats to eat

Show the children some seaside treats such as rock, candyfloss and seafood. Talk about the nutritional value of these and allow the children the chance to make card replicas. Such treats became popular with the development of sea front shops.

3 Seaside gifts

Children can look at artefacts like the ones in the photograph below and then respond to questions such as: Where do you think these holiday gifts have come from? What are they made from? Who in your family would you give them to?

Resources

Card; paper; paints and painting materials; tissue; Cellophane; paper paste; fabric; scissors; PVA glue; long strips of paper for friezes; plastic foam; wire; wire cutters; postcard-size card

Historical elements

vocabulary of passing time ✓
differences between times ✓
experience the past as shown in
    pictures/writing/TV etc. ✓
asking/answering questions ✓
stories ✓
communicating work ✓

4 Punch and Judy

This famous puppet show was introduced into Britain at the beginning of the 19th century and became a popular seaside entertainment. The children can try making their own puppets.

A present from the seaside

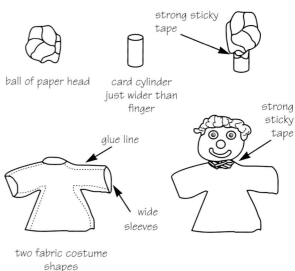

strong sticky tape

ball of paper head

card cylinder just wider than finger

glue line

wide sleeves

two fabric costume shapes

strong sticky tape

Further activities

1 Stories of the sea

Read the children stories from the past that concern the sea, e.g. Grace Darling's act of heroism, or the story of the *Titanic*.

2 Seaside model

Help the children to make a class seaside model. This can then be embellished with model buildings, shops and people in different periods.

3 Postcards

Try to obtain some postcards of seaside scenes in the past. Display these and invite the children to make their own. The children can use brown felt-tipped pens to create a sepia-like effect. To 'age' the card, overwash with a coating of cold strong tea and allow to dry.

4 Tourists

Contact the tourist information centre in a nearby seaside town. Find out how many tourists have visited over a period of years. Where have tourists stayed? What did they spend their time doing? Draw tourists of today and compare them with a traveller from about 1900, looking at items such as swimwear and luggage.

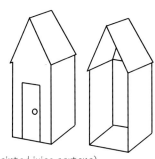

esplanade (mosaic blocks or rubbings)

hotels (cartons)

sand (on sugar paper)

pier (soft wire covered with paper)

sea (fabric)

beach huts (painted juice cartons)

Buildings

First activities

1 Our school

Allow the children to inspect the school buildings, find out how old they are, and draw pictures of them. The children can then visit another local school that was built at a different time and in a different architectural style and do drawings there. (It may be possible to arrange exchange visits.)

2 Castles and big houses

Take the children to visit a large house or castle in the area. Look carefully at what life would have been like in this building long ago. Use large cartons and 'stone' prints the children have made to create a model of the building visited.

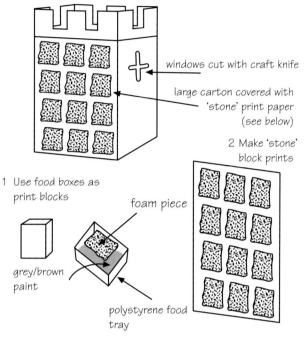

windows cut with craft knife

large carton covered with 'stone' print paper (see below)

2 Make 'stone' block prints

1 Use food boxes as print blocks

foam piece

grey/brown paint

polystyrene food tray

Why were castles built ?

Who do you think lived in a castle ?

Historical elements

chronology ✓
vocabulary of passing time ✓
differences between times ✓
experience the past as shown in pictures/writing/TV etc. ✓
stories ✓
communicating work ✓

Resources

Paper; crayons; pencils; felt-tipped pens; large sheets of paper; large cartons (washing machine or TV boxes are ideal); boxes (food packaging); food trays; Artstraws; Cellophane; foam pieces; poster paints

Further activities

1 Public buildings

Choose two or three important buildings in the vicinity of the school. Allow the children to look at the buildings closely. Ask the children to make models of these buildings, using junk modelling materials.

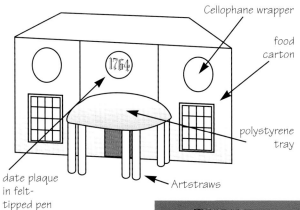

Cellophane wrapper

food carton

1764

polystyrene tray

date plaque in felt-tipped pen

Artstraws

2 Places in stories of the past

Tell the children about some important buildings in British history such as the Tower of London, Hampton Court Palace and Hadrian's Wall. The children can inspect pictures of these buildings and then draw their own pictures of them to illustrate their writing.

3 Building materials

Allow the children to examine samples of building materials. Point out that wood and mud were used to make buildings many centuries ago. Tell the children how bricks and tiles are made, and where slate comes from. Contrast these with other building materials such as breeze blocks. Ask the children to try to replicate the surface texture and shades of colour found in the materials, using coloured pencils and pastels.

4 Building decoration

Give the children the chance to look at decorative aspects of buildings such as arches and doorways, stained glass windows, ornaments and gargoyles, and make drawings of them.

-nothing

Being a child

First activities

1 Babies now and then
Talk to the children about babies they know - brothers, sisters, relations, or babies of family friends. Discuss what a baby's day is like, and the clothes and equipment babies need now. Contrast this with times past.

Resources

Paper; crayons; felt-tipped pens; charcoal; pastels; large sheets of paper; paints and painting materials

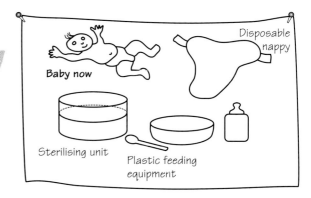

Baby now

Disposable nappy

Sterilising unit

Plastic feeding equipment

Pottery bowl

Baby wrapped in swaddling clothes

Wooden spoon

Baby then

2 Children at work
In the past most children in Britain were expected to work. During the 19th century, working conditions were very bad and young children worked long hours. Show the children pictures of young workers in factories and mines. The children can draw their own pictures, using charcoal or pastels.

3 Good girls and boys
Ask the children about the rules they have at home concerning behaviour. Discuss what the school rules say about how they should behave. Compare these with the expectations of children in the past. Help the children to create illustrated lists of rules for now and 100 years ago.

School rules 1999

Do not run indoors

Be quiet in the hall

word-processed list

Being good in 1899

Be quiet
Speak only when spoken to
Stand up to speak to an adult

handwritten list

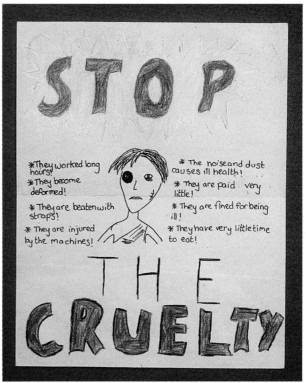

STOP

* They worked long hours!
* They become deformed!
* They are beaten with straps!
* They are injured by the machines!

* The noise and dust causes ill health!
* They are paid very little!
* They are fined for being ill!
* They have very little time to eat!

THE CRUELTY

Further activities

1 Another era

Choose another time in history and help the class find out all they can about children then. Make a large class picture of children from the period. Information can be written around it.

2 Story children

Read aloud passages involving children from books such as *Oliver Twist* and *The Treasure Seekers*. Ask the children to compare and draw these characters.

3 Clues in paintings

Look at some paintings depicting children and ask the class to comment on them. The class can then make drawings of parts of the paintings.

Historical elements

chronology ✔
vocabulary of passing time ✔
differences between times ✔
using sources ✔
asking/answering questions ✔
stories ✔
communicating work ✔

Children from another time

First activities

1 Staple foods now and long ago

Discuss what a staple food is and tell the children that some of the foods we eat every day were not available to people several centuries ago. Ask the children to draw pictures of some staple foods. These can be put on display.

People used to eat bread

We eat bread, pasta, rice and potatoes

People used to drink ale (beer)

We drink beer, tea and coffee

2 Cooking food

Discuss the means by which food has been cooked over the centuries. Find pictures and accounts of the cooking of food. Ask the children to work in groups, painting card pieces black. They can assemble the black pieces to make images of fireplaces and stoves from the past. Compare these with the appliances we use today.

3 Foods from the 'New World'

Assemble samples of foods that were introduced into Britain by explorers. Include the potato and coffee. Tell the children about some of these voyagers, e.g. Sir Walter Raleigh. The children can write a chronicle of his life and draw some samples.

4 Keeping food fresh

Examine some of the foods we eat, and talk about the ways in which they are kept 'fresh'. Discuss refrigeration, freezing and vacuum packing. Tell the children that before people had these ways of keeping food, they used methods such as smoking, salting and drying. Investigate and draw pictures to show how this was done.

Try drying apple rings. Space the rings out along a string and keep away from bright light and smells.

Model foods from the past
Which do you think were eaten at a party?

raised pie
flan
jelly
Pork or bacon
pie
Harvest loaf and plait
marzipan fruits

Cooking on a fire

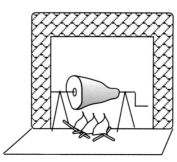

Using a spit

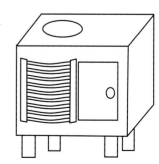

A kitchen range

• Use red and yellow tissue paper for fires
• Use black painted card for pots, spit, stove

Further activities

1 Mrs Beeton

Ask the class to find out who Mrs Beeton was and when she lived. They can draw pictures of her and copy and annotate recipes from her famous book.

2 A diarist's meals

Children can look in the diaries of people from the past to find their accounts of meals they have eaten. Examples might include the diaries of Samuel Pepys or *The Diary of a Nobody*. The children can draw or paint the foods that were on the menu.

3 Medieval banquet

Research the kinds of foods eaten at a special meal in medieval times. The children can then make playdough replica foods, which can be painted and varnished and set out for toys dressed in appropriate costumes.

Historical elements

vocabulary of passing time ✓
differences between times ✓
experience the past as shown in
    pictures/writing/TV etc. ✓
using sources ✓
asking/answering questions ✓
eyewitness accounts ✓
communicating work ✓

Resources

Large sheets of sugar paper; pencils; crayons; felt-tipped pens; black paint; large brushes; red and yellow tissue paper; PVA glue; apples; string; playdough; paints and varnish

Transport

Can you find out when people rode around in these?

First activities

1 Horses

Assemble a range of sources showing the children how horses have been used as a means of transport through the ages. Ask the children to work in groups, sponge-printing a row of horses. They can then cut out and stick down the horses and add people, carts, etc. to make a picture.

2 Water travel

Talk about the kinds of boats people made in the distant past. Make model boats and test out size and shape features. Look for pictures of boats from a particular era. Visit a boat museum, or a famous ship like the *Mary Rose* or the *Cutty Sark*, and make a class display. If the school is near a canal, look at the importance of canals in Britain in the 18th and 19th centuries. Make model narrow boats from card. Paint these in traditional colours.

3 Model cars

Ask the children to bring into school model vintage cars. Display and research these so they can be placed on a timeline. Individual children can study, draw and write about a vehicle they particularly like.

4 Bikes

If possible, ask one of the children to bring his or her bike into the classroom and use it as the stimulus for talking about the history of the bicycle. Precut a large number of wheels of different sizes from black paper. Invite the children to work in pairs or groups, using the wheels to create one of the bicycles below.

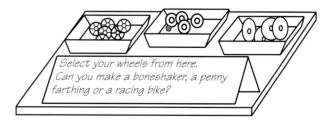

Select your wheels from here.
Can you make a boneshaker, a penny farthing or a racing bike?

Further activities

1 Speed

Talk with the class about the importance of making journeys as short as possible. Compare how long a journey by carriage may have taken with the same journey by car now. Create a scale of distances travelled by various means in the same time.

2 Road-making and road networks

The Romans built some of the most direct roads in Britain. Ask the children to find information on how the Romans created a road surface, and the routes their roads took. Compare this with road-building today. With adult help, the children can use materials such as brick, hard core, sand or Polyfilla to create a model of the 'layers' in ancient and modern roads.

3 The railways

Discuss railway journeys that the children have made. Visit a railway museum or research the story of particular trains such as Stephenson's 'Rocket' or 'The Flying Scotsman'. Create large wall paintings of these.

Resources

Poster paints; polystyrene trays; plastic foam pieces; junk model packaging; PVA glue; scissors; sugar paper; hard core; brick fragments; sand; gravel; Polyfilla

Historical elements

vocabulary of passing time ✓
differences between times ✓
experience the past as shown in
    pictures/writing/TV etc. ✓
asking/answering questions ✓
communicating work ✓

Going to work

First activities

1 On the farm

Discuss with the children what we mean by work, and the kinds of jobs people do nowadays. Then focus on work on the land and look for pictures of people farming from medieval times to the present day. Ask the children to draw pictures showing hand tools and horse-drawn machines, which can be placed alongside pictures of modern tractors to create a gallery.

A horse-drawn plough   A modern tractor

2 Butcher, baker and candlestick maker

Invite groups within the class to look at how modern shopkeepers carry out their work, the kinds of tools they use and how their working day compares with that of workers in the past. Make a display of their findings.

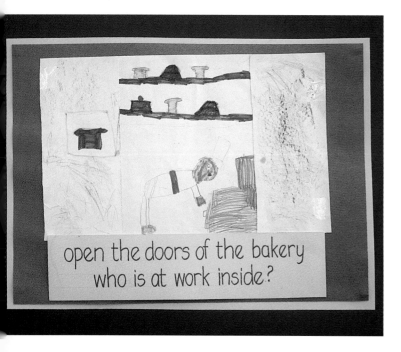

open the doors of the bakery who is at work inside?

3 Crafts

Describe to the children some of the jobs traditionally done by craftsmen and women. Ask them to find out what a cobbler does, and why there are so few blacksmiths today. If there is a potter's wheel in school, allow the children to try it. Help them to work with clay and modelling tools. Show the children some coarse woven cloth, and allow them to inspect it under a magnifier. They will see how the threads are twisted around one another. The children can try weaving, using homemade looms.

A shoebox loom

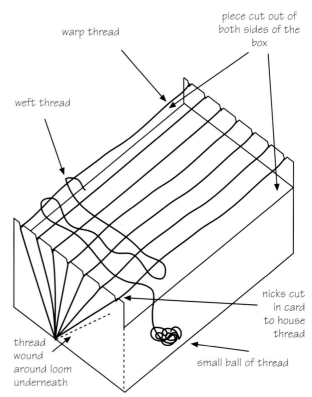

warp thread

piece cut out of both sides of the box

weft thread

nicks cut in card to house thread

thread wound around loom underneath

small ball of thread

Historical elements

chronology ✓
vocabulary of passing time ✓
differences between times ✓
using sources ✓
asking/answering questions ✓
communicating work ✓

Further activities

1 Working hours

Look at the number of hours worked by people in Britain in the 19th century. The children can make giant clock faces showing these times.

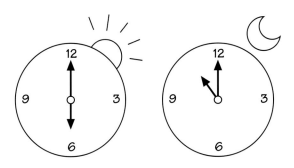

100 years ago people in Britain worked very long hours in factories and mines. Servants worked these hours too.

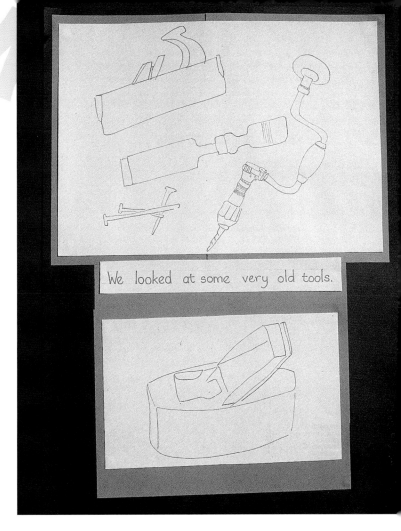

We looked at some very old tools.

An Edwardian nanny's day

Up at 6 a.m. to make the fires

Get the children's breakfast

Walk to the park

Clean the nursery

Mend the children's clothes

Talk about what other tasks nanny did every day

2 A day in the life of...

Trace a day in the life of a domestic servant such as a housekeeper or an errand boy in Britain in the Edwardian era. As a class, make a frieze of pictures showing the jobs the servant had to do.

3 Tools and technology

Choose a job and investigate how the tools associated with it have changed in the last 50 years. For example, a joiner can now use power tools and an office worker can use a word processor and a calculator. Use old tool catalogues to put together a montage, which can then be displayed on the classroom wall next to drawings of old tools.

Resources

Paper; crayons; chalks; felt-tipped pens; papers of various weights; clay and modelling tools; weaving cards or homemade looms with yarn; large card circles for clock faces; old catalogues showing power tools; frieze paper

Famous people

First activities

1 Royalty

Discuss with the children why kings and queens are important and famous. Help the children to find out about British monarchs of the past. A 'family', e.g. the Plantagenets or the Tudors, could be chosen or one king or queen could be studied in detail. A thumbnail biography could be compiled, listing the monarch's reign dates, the names of his or her parents, and some of the important events in his or her life. Find likenesses of the people studied and make busts of them, using air-drying clay.

2 Robbers and scoundrels

Research some of the people in the past who were notorious. You might choose highwaymen (or highwaywomen). The children can make a paper and card collage of some of these characters waiting to hold up a stagecoach. To make 'foliage' for camouflage, add washing-up liquid to green paint and put a small quantity in a yoghurt pot. Place paper over the top and blow down a straw into the liquid. As the mixture bubbles up it makes patterns on the paper. These can be cut out and added to the trees in the collage. The children can also create 'wanted' posters, using information they have about the wrongdoings.

3 Workers for children

Find out about the life of Baden-Powell and the history of the Scout movement, or the work done by Dr Barnardo, or the life and work of someone in local history whose name has been given to an organisation or building used for the care of children. Allow the children to write and illustrate a class biography to put in the book corner.

green 'bubble' foliage

black fabric cloak

card coach covered in black paper

stencil-printed horses

Resources

Clay; clay paints; wool; varnish; newsprint; sugar paper; paper glue; poster paints; pastels; PVA glue; tissue paper; card; scissors; shoeboxes or similar cartons; felt-tipped pens

Further activities

1 Soldiers and sailors

Find out about the exploits of someone like Horatio Nelson, the Duke of Wellington, or Sir Francis Drake. Invite the children to work in pairs, creating at one end of a shoebox a scene enacting an event in the soldier or sailor's life. A hole can then be cut at the other end so that a little peep-show is made.

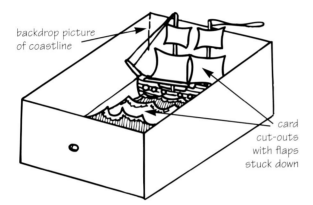

backdrop picture of coastline

card cut-outs with flaps stuck down

2 Designers and artists

Choose one or two designers or artists from the past. Look at reproductions of their work. Try out their techniques and replicate some of their motifs and designs. For example, if the children look at the work of William Morris, they can inspect fabric and wallpaper samples and draw or trace some of the flower and bird motifs.

3 William Shakespeare

Create a topic web of questions about William Shakespeare, and then set about finding the answers. Mount a class display of drawings and a model of the Globe theatre.

Historical elements

chronology ✓
vocabulary of passing time ✓
differences between times ✓
experience the past as shown in
    pictures/writing/TV etc. ✓
using sources ✓
asking/answering questions ✓
communicating work ✓

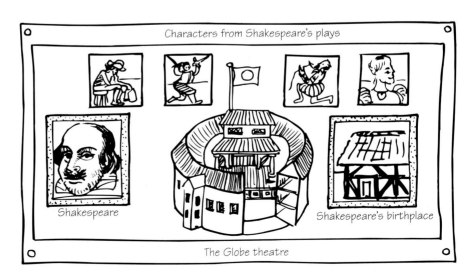

Characters from Shakespeare's plays

Shakespeare

Shakespeare's birthplace

The Globe theatre

Money and shops

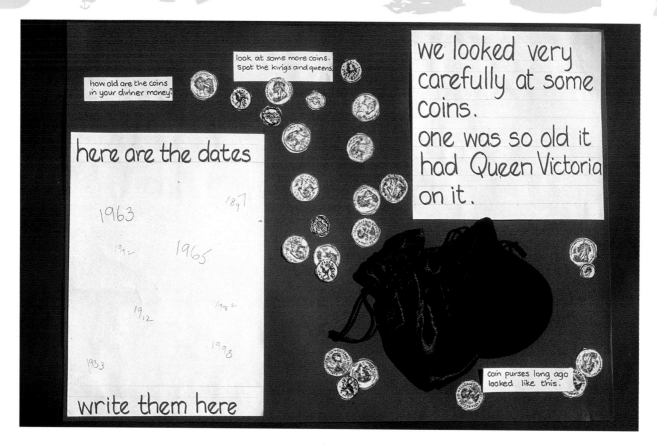

how old are the coins in your dinner money?

look at some more coins. spot the kings and queens!

we looked very carefully at some coins.
one was so old it had Queen Victoria on it.

here are the dates

1963
1897
1992
1965
19,2
199,2
1998
1933

write them here

coin purses long ago looked like this.

First activities

1 Markets

People have exchanged and sold goods at markets for many hundreds of years. Find out about markets of the past and the kinds of goods sold. Choose a period of history and ask the children to set up a market stall in the classroom 'selling' replica goods. Using cartons, paper or fabric, allow the children to make their own model market stalls. These can be arranged on a display table to make market day.

2 Coins

Examine modern, pre-decimal, and earlier (if available) British coins. Ask the children to search out an important event attached to the date each coin was minted. Make rubbings with lightweight paper and soft crayon.

3 Shop signs

Shopkeepers still place signs over their shops, but in the past all signs showed the kinds of goods for sale or the services on offer. Find pictures of old signs, and then ask the children to create their own with dowel or pea sticks.

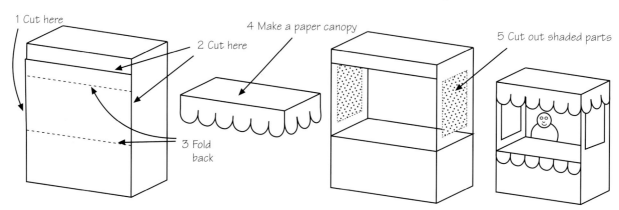

1 Cut here
2 Cut here
3 Fold back
4 Make a paper canopy
5 Cut out shaded parts

Further activities

1 The cost of the shopping

Assemble food packs and wrappers and place them in a shopping basket. Ask the children to find out the price of each item nowadays. Compare today's prices with a price list for long ago and create a comparative display.

2 Advertising

Ask the children to cut out some advertisements from magazines. Compare these with advertisements from long ago.

3 Banknotes

Show the children some current British banknotes. Allow them to examine the notes with magnifiers. Talk about how it is made difficult for forgers to copy banknotes. In groups, the children can make large pictures of each side of each note. These can be displayed and annotated with questions and the children's answers.

Historical elements

chronology ✓
vocabulary of passing time ✓
differences between times ✓
using sources ✓
asking/answering questions ✓
communicating work ✓

Resources

Soft crayons (gold, silver and brown are good for coin rubbings); cartons (e.g. cereal packs); scissors; paper; felt-tipped pens; card; paper clips; dowel or pea sticks; paper fasteners; paints and painting materials; sugar paper; magazines containing advertisements

Entertainment

First activities

1 Joker
Find out about jesters, jokers and entertainers in history. Collect images of jesters in costume. Allow the children to find out about court entertainment, street players, and the history of the circus.

2 Music making
Use an old instrument as a stimulus to a discussion of what instruments are made from and how they are played. Allow the children to talk about signs of age in objects of the past. They can then draw the instrument.

3 Singing
Collect and learn traditional songs, and record when they were written. Create a display of choir singers, each with the words of a song (ancient or modern) attached.

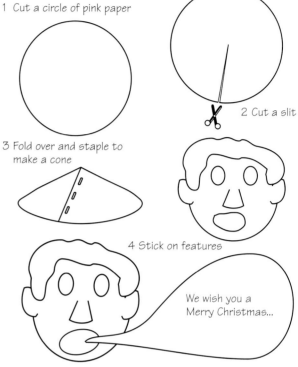

1 Cut a circle of pink paper

2 Cut a slit

3 Fold over and staple to make a cone

4 Stick on features

We wish you a Merry Christmas...

5 Write out songs for singers to 'sing'

Further activities

1 Moving pictures - the cinema

Talk about the children's own experiences of going to the cinema, and discuss the popularity of the cinema before the advent of television. Some of the children may have elderly relatives who can tell of their trips to the cinema. Explain the process by which we see moving pictures on the cinema screen and give the children the opportunity to make 'flicker' books.

2 TV

Create a display about the history of television in Britain. The children can ask their parents and grandparents what their favourite programmes were. They can compile a list of old and new children's viewing. They can look for the number of families in Britain with a TV set in each decade, the date of the introduction of colour television, and the start dates of different TV channels.

Historical elements

chronology ✓
differences between times ✓
experience the past as shown in
    pictures/writing/TV etc. ✓
using sources ✓
asking/answering questions ✓
communicating work ✓

3 The story of an instrument

Allow each work group to choose a different instrument, and then draw a timeline and example pictures of the instrument and its predecessors.

Resources

Coloured paper; scissors; paints; felt-tipped pens; white paper for flicker books; black card; bottle tops; PVA glue

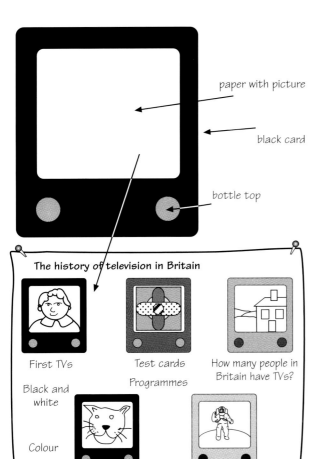

paper with picture

black card

bottle top

The history of television in Britain

First TVs

Test cards

Programmes

How many people in Britain have TVs?

Black and white

Colour

Celebrations

First activities

1 Happy birthday

List the birthday of every child in the class. Then give each child a chart of months, and ask them to fill in the birthday of everyone in their family, with help at home. Assemble information about the years in which family members were born. Give the children practice in using the vocabulary of time, by asking key questions such as: Who was born before...? Does Anna's birthday come before or after Joe's? Who was alive when Queen Elizabeth II was crowned?

Ask the children what other events are celebrated in their family. Collect a list of events. Choose one, e.g. a christening, and find out the customs that were common in these ceremonies in the past. Help the children to make a class book of this information.

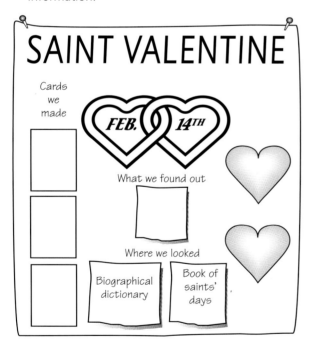

2 Saints' days

Find out the stories of the lives of St George, St David and St Patrick and other saints whose names have been given to local schools and the local church, or saints' names that are common in the area. Write up the stories and facts and decorate them with a border indicating the cause to which the saint in dedicated, e.g. St Christopher's border could be a trail of travellers.

3 Christmas

Find out about some of the customs attached to Christmas present and past, and the dates they began. Here are some examples: the Christmas tree; the yule log; carol-singing in the street; a Christmas 'box'; Boxing Day; the sending of Christmas cards. Make a concertina display of pictures and writing.

Historical elements

chronology ✔
vocabulary of passing time ✔
experience the past as shown in
    pictures/writing/TV etc. ✔
using sources ✔
asking/answering questions ✔
stories ✔
eyewitness accounts ✔
communicating work ✔

Further activities

1 Guy Fawkes

Talk to the children about the events surrounding the Gunpowder Plot. Ask them to write an account of the story from the point of view of one of the conspirators, or of a royalist sympathiser. Make a model guy and display him alongside firework safety rules and the children's writing.

2 Local events

Find out about local celebrations, their history and what happens. Look in the local newspaper archive at the library and at books about local history for information. There may be events around May Day, Shrove Tuesday or locally developed celebrations such as well-dressing. The story can be enacted by the children. They can record their work for a display to which local dignitaries and the children's parents can be invited.

• Mark in relevant festivals for the class
• Attach children's symbols to each date

Resources

Paper; card; crayons; felt-tipped pens; tissue paper; paper doilies; paints and painting materials; frieze paper

3 A calendar of celebrations

Make a class calendar of events celebrated by the children on different days of the year. Be sure to include celebrations from different cultures. Ask the children to draw symbols to attach to each day. Display as a frieze right around the room.

Romans

First activities

1 Numbers and words

Show the children Roman numerals in dates and on clock faces, and make a chart of what they mean. Ask the children to draw Roman numerals on decorative clock faces. Investigate some Latin words in the English language.

2 What they wore

Find pictures of Roman togas, tunics and sandals. Make a toga and allow children to try it on.

Making and wearing a Roman toga

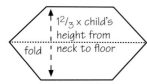

$1\frac{2}{3}$ x child's height from neck to floor

fold

3 x child's height from neck to floor

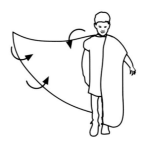

3 Jewellery

Inspect fragments of Roman jewellery in a museum or in history picture books. Make some items featuring similar patterns from Newclay or playdough, and when dry wrap them in silver or gold foil.

36

Further activities

1 Local evidence

Look at local maps to see if the school is near one of the main roads built in Britain by the Romans. Contact local museums to find out where the nearest Roman archaeological remains are held. Allow the children to inspect these. If the children can view Roman mosaics, they can try making a mosaic from pebbles set in Newclay or Polyfilla.

2 Roman weapons

Find out about the weapons carried by a Roman soldier, and some of the bigger Roman instruments of war. These can be modelled using construction sets such as Meccano or Lego, or made from craft materials with adult help.

3 Resisting the invasion

The widow of the leader of the Iceni (a Celtic tribe in ancient Britain), led her people against the Romans. Seek out images of Boadicea or Boudicca and copy them.

Historical elements

chronology ✔
particular periods and societies ✔
representations of the past ✔
using sources ✔
asking/answering questions ✔
using historical terms ✔
communicating work ✔

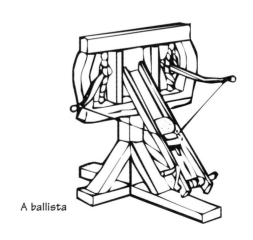

A ballista

37

Anglo-Saxons

First activities

1 Who were the Anglo-Saxons?
With the children's help, make a large map of northern Europe and trace where the Anglo-Saxons came from. Mark their routes to Britain and where they settled with wool and pins.

2 Farming
Look at and replicate pictures of Anglo-Saxon farming methods. Find out what Anglo-Saxons grew and what they liked to eat.

3 Having fun
These people probably had little time to spare, but there were feast days where there would have been music and entertainments. Find pictures and replicate them. Jointed figures can be made with paper fasteners at the joins so that the figures will move. Alternatively, outlines of people can be sketched with felt-tipped pens and then painted in with watercolour paints.

4 Homes
Find artists' interpretations of what Anglo-Saxon homes looked like. Allow the children to make model replicas, using clay and twigs.

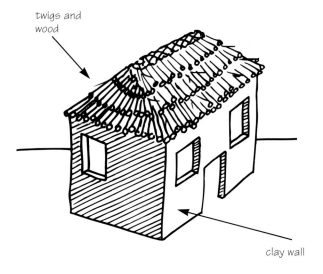

twigs and wood

clay wall

Further activities

1 Alfred the Great

Alfred is the only king of Britain to have had 'the Great' added to his name. Ask the children to research the source of this reputation and Alfred's many achievements. Make individual concertina books or a class one, with each fold featuring work on a different aspect of Alfred's life.

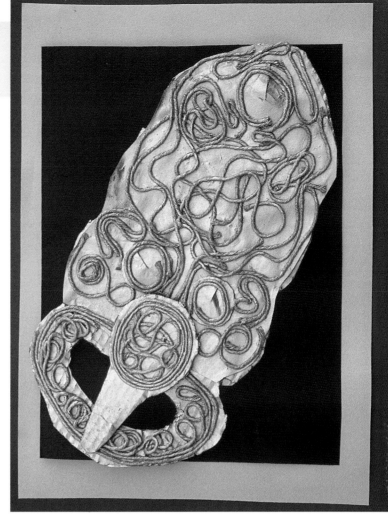

2 Christianity

Saxon settlers were pagan, but they were converted to the Christian faith by missionaries around the sixth century. There are many Saxon churches still standing. Take the children to visit one, looking particularly at the style and shapes in the building. Give the children card templates of some of the predominant shapes and ask them to create a drawing of a church with Saxon features.

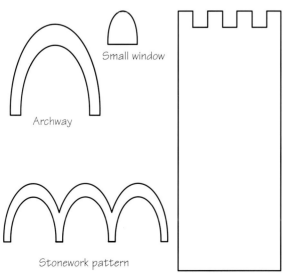

Small window

Archway

Stonework pattern

Church tower front

3 Sutton Hoo and other finds

The grave of a Saxon king was excavated at Sutton Hoo in Suffolk and many objects were discovered. Find pictures of these and discuss with the children what they tell us about the king and his followers.

Historical elements

chronology ✓
particular periods and societies ✓
representations of the past ✓
using sources ✓
asking/answering questions ✓
using historical terms ✓
communicating work ✓

Resources

Large sheets of paper; wool and pins; twigs and brushwood; clay; felt-tipped pens; paper fasteners; watercolour paints; PVA glue; card; string; gold foil or gold paint

39

Vikings

First activities

1 Ships

The Vikings were famous warriors and shipbuilders. Find out how their ships were constructed and make a model.

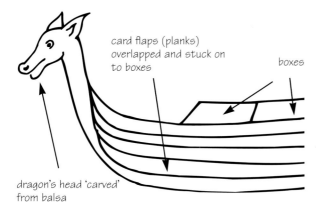

card flaps (planks) overlapped and stuck on to boxes

boxes

dragon's head 'carved' from balsa

2 Fighting

Viking soldiers wore distinctive helmets. The children could make models of these. Start with a balloon base, which can be half covered in paper strips dipped in glue. When completely dry, pop the balloon and cut the edges of the helmet to neaten them before painting.

3 Everyday clothes

Look for pictures of Viking clothes. The men are often depicted wearing trousers and a loose shirt, and the women in a dress with a kind of tabard on top. Vikings used dyes from natural sources. Try dyeing fabrics in class, using onion skins, blackberries, or other fruits or vegetables. (For example, avocado skins produce a pink colour.)

1 Steep onion skins in boiling water

2 Leave to cool, then strain off liquid

3 Soak fabric in liquid overnight

4 Wring out and allow to dry

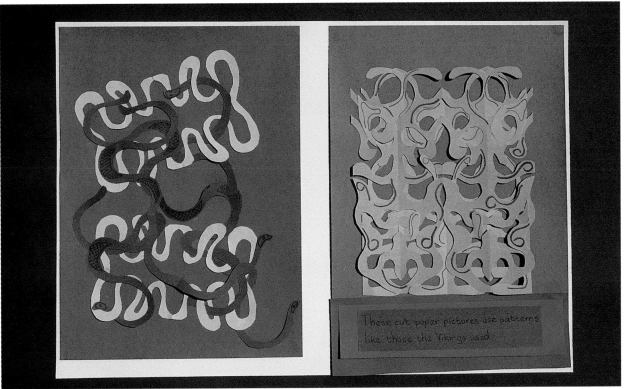

These cut paper pictures use patterns like those the Vikings used.

Further activities

1 Patterns and decoration
Look at pictures of Viking artefacts to decipher the elaborate patterns used. Replicate these patterns, using cut paper or paint.

2 Erik the Viking
Read a story from Terry Jones' book *Erik the Viking* to the children. Ask them to choose a part of the story to write about and illustrate.

Displaying a frieze

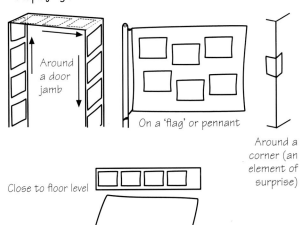

Around a door jamb

On a 'flag' or pennant

Around a corner (an element of surprise)

Close to floor level

Resources

Card; scissors; paints and painting materials; balsa wood; cotton sheeting; onion skins; vegetables/fruits (e.g. blackberries) to use for dye; boiling water or access to a stove; rubber gloves; a washing line and clothes pegs; frieze paper; paper glue; felt-tipped pens

Historical elements

chronology ✔
vocabulary of passing time ✔
particular periods and societies ✔
representations of the past ✔
using sources ✔
asking/answering questions ✔
using historical terms ✔
communicating work ✔

The Tudors

First activities

1 The Tudor rose

Seek out images of this emblem of the royal Tudor family. Make drawings or potato-cut patterns of the rose to decorate project books and displays.

- Make potato cuts of parts of the Tudor rose and print

3 Timeline

Make a timeline to fit along one whole wall of the classroom. Mark the ends 1480 and 1605, as the children need from 1485 to 1603 to mark the reigns of the Tudors. The children can then attach dates and other information to the timeline.

Historical elements

chronology ✓
vocabulary of passing time ✓
particular periods and societies ✓
representations of the past ✓
using sources ✓
asking/answering questions ✓
using historical terms ✓
communicating work ✓

2 Monarchs

Allow the children to work in groups to find out about one of the Tudor monarchs. As well as accessing books and CD-ROMs, the children can look at reproductions of famous paintings and try to interpret what they see, both in drawings and in writing. Annotate the reproductions with questions such as: Why do you think Holbein painted Henry VIII full-length like this? Look carefully at what Henry is wearing. What are your impressions?

Further activities

1 Palaces and other buildings

Visit or find out about one of the royal palaces, or a large house of this period near to the school. The children can then make drawings and learn about the construction and interior furnishings.

2 Costume

Inspect, trace and draw pictures of royal costumes from the Tudor period. Discuss the fabrics used, where they came from and how they were made. Point out the importance of colour in Tudor royal costumes, the 'richness' of the fabric and the decoration.

3 Ships

Study either the trade routes and cargo ships of this period, or the warships and battles fought. For example, the children can find out about the raising of the *Mary Rose*, or about the Spanish Armada. Make a card cutaway model of a warship or a cargo ship.

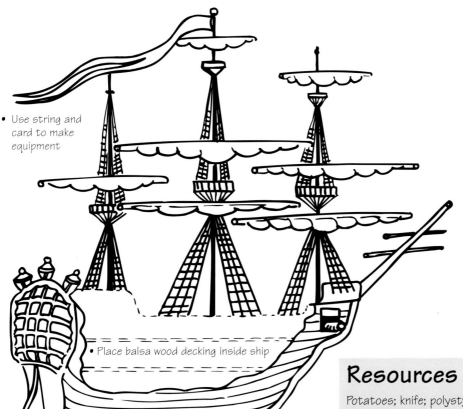

• Use string and card to make equipment

• Place balsa wood decking inside ship

• Make barrels from bottle tops

paper dipped in paper glue wound around bottle top

bottle top

more paper wrapped around centre to make barrel shape

Resources

Potatoes; knife; polystyrene trays; foam pieces; poster paints; paper; white card; felt-tipped pens; brown card; balsa wood; bottle tops; card and string scraps; paper glue; PVA glue; scissors

The rich in Tudor times

First activities

1 Homes

Make models of Tudor buildings from card, adding other materials to show points of architectural style.

2 Evidence in paintings

Look at paintings of the Tudor period to find clues to the way of life of the rich. It may be possible to see pastimes such as hunting, falconry, music and embroidery, and to spot toys, furniture and other objects. These can be drawn and added to a 'Tudor portfolio'.

3 Costumes

Find out about styles of the period and make a ruff. Dress a child in period costume and ask the other children in the class to draw him or her. Discuss what these clothes would have been like to wear for everyday activities.

Historical elements

chronology ✔
vocabulary of passing time ✔
particular periods and societies ✔
representations of the past ✔
using sources ✔
asking/answering questions ✔
using historical terms ✔
communicating work ✔

Making a ruff

1 Cut a strip of fabric 50 cm x 6 cm

2 Cut 3 long rectangles of lining fabric, spray with starch

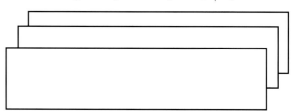

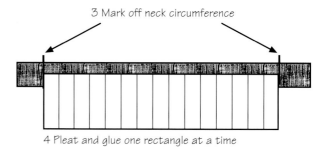

3 Mark off neck circumference

4 Pleat and glue one rectangle at a time

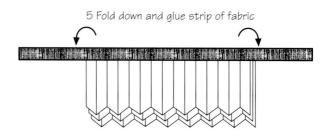

5 Fold down and glue strip of fabric

Further activities

1 Pomanders and pot pourri

It is said that these were used to scent rooms and ward off evil smells. Let some oranges dry out for two weeks. Put masking tape around the middle of the orange in both directions. Using a blunt needle, make holes on the exposed part of the orange so that whole cloves can be pressed in. Sprinkle cinnamon on the orange, wrap it in foil and store for six weeks. Then remove the tape and tie ribbon in its place.

For pot pourri, put into a bowl 50g each of whole cloves, ground cinnamon, ground nutmeg, allspice, and borax. Add 450g salt and pieces of orange or lemon peel. Mix well.

ribbon

orange

cloves

A pomander

2 Facts and figures

Ask the children to find out some data about the rich in Tudor times. Give them some 'starter' questions on a display, together with reference books. The questions should relate to household size, budgets, how time was spent and the jobs people did. The children can then set out some questions for their classmates to try and answer.

Resources

Boxes; paper; paper glue; balsa wood sheets; black and white paint; lolly sticks; white lining fabric; spray starch; fabric scissors; PVA glue; oranges; whole cloves; ground cinnamon, allspice, cloves and nutmeg; sticky tape; coloured ribbon; blunt needle; silver foil; borax; orange or lemon peel; salt

The poor in Tudor times

First activities

1 Being poor

Before accessing any sources of information, ask the children to help formulate ideas about what they need to find out about the poor in Tudor times. The children can write up their questions on a big chart and then go into groups to try to find answers.

2 Trades

Unemployment was high in Tudor times and some tradespeople, even though they may have served an apprenticeship, still found it difficult to get work. Find out the range of trades in Tudor times and make a large web display showing what the trade was called, what the tradesperson did, and what service this provided.

3 Eating to live

The diet of the poor was meagre and comprised mainly vegetables. Ask the children to find out and draw some of the things eaten. These can be mounted in a big display, with a large cooking pot and the foodstuffs cut out and pinned against the pot.

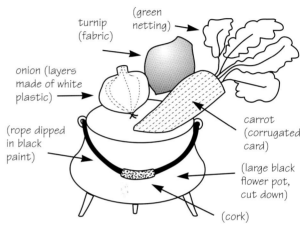

turnip (fabric)

(green netting)

onion (layers made of white plastic)

carrot (corrugated card)

(rope dipped in black paint)

(large black flower pot, cut down)

(cork)

Further activities

1 Punishment

The penalties for pickpocketing or other minor crimes were often harsh. Ask the children to find out what could happen to a person who, for example, stole a sheep. Make a working model of a pillory or stocks.

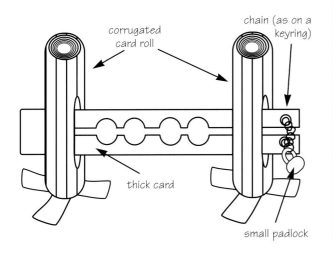

corrugated card roll

chain (as on a keyring)

thick card

small padlock

2 Health

The poor lived in conditions where illness and disease were rife. Help the children to paint a Tudor street scene, with the nearest house 'cut away' to reveal the interior. Flaps can then be cut in the picture and behind each flap a hazard to health can be listed.

flap

flap

3 Clues to servant life

Using books, pictures and information from CD-ROMs, the children can describe a day in the life of a servant in a big house, or a man who is looking for work, or a woman who does mending at home to earn money for the family.

We know more about diseases and how our bodies work nowadays.

keeping clean prevents infection

fleas carry disease

rats carry disease

coughs and sneezes bring diseases

Historical elements

chronology ✓
vocabulary of passing time ✓
particular periods and societies ✓
representations of the past ✓
using sources ✓
asking/answering questions ✓
using historical terms ✓
communicating work ✓

Resources

Large sheet of display paper; large felt-tipped pens; card; paper; corrugated card; paper fasteners; poster paints

Victorians and 'progress'

First activities

1 Factories

Study old photographs and pictures of industrial landscapes and factories in the Victorian era. Discuss the likely working conditions and quality of life of the workers. Using pens, brushes and washable black ink, give the children the opportunity to try pen and ink drawing techniques. Make a composite industrial landscape scene from the children's efforts.

2 Inventions

Choose something that was invented in Victorian times for each work group in the class, and give the children the resources to find out about it. Place their drawings and writing on a timeline.

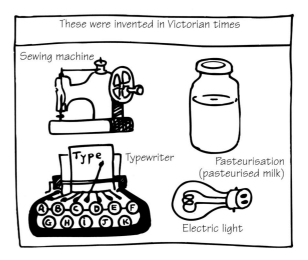

These were invented in Victorian times

Sewing machine

Typewriter

Pasteurisation (pasteurised milk)

Electric light

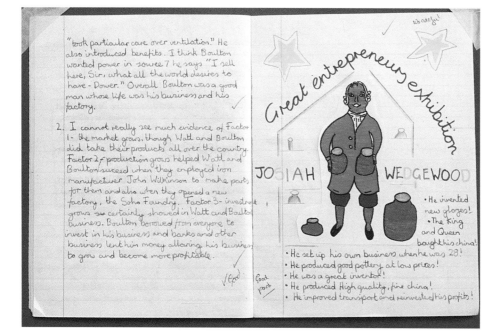

3 Schooling

Find out about changes in the school day of a British child in the 1830s and the 1890s. Look at education and the law, and the effects this had on children's school experience. List the things in the classroom that may not have been there in Victorian times. Display these on replica slates or on large blackboards.

Further activities

1 Queen Victoria

Make a portrait of Queen Victoria. Place a slightly flattened ball of paper on to a large piece of card. Dip strips of paper into paper glue and lay them across the paper ball, anchoring it to the card. 'Build' a nose and cheeks. Allow the model to dry out completely before painting. Add paper or wool hair and a fabric headdress. Stick on sequins to make the jewellery.

2 The Great Exhibition

The Great Exhibition of 1851 was a celebration of Britain's 'progress' and achievement. Look carefully at pictures of the Crystal Palace before making a model, using black card strips and Cellophane. Discuss some of the things that the Victorians placed on show there.

3 Nursing

The children can trace the history of the nursing profession and compare conditions in, for example, the Crimean War, with those in hospitals today. A paper collage of Florence Nightingale can be set alongside the children's pictures and writing.

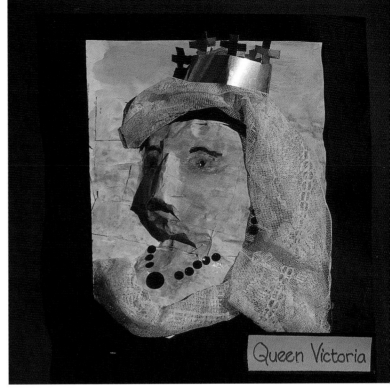

Queen Victoria

'The lady of the lamp'

Nursing today

Historical elements

chronology ✓
vocabulary of passing time ✓
particular periods and societies ✓
representations of the past ✓
using sources ✓
asking/answering questions ✓
reasons and results ✓
using historical terms ✓
communicating work ✓

Resources

Washable black ink, pens and brushes; felt-tipped pens; black paper; white paper; paper glue; fabric; paint and painting materials; sequins; beads; Cellophane; black card; yellow tissue paper

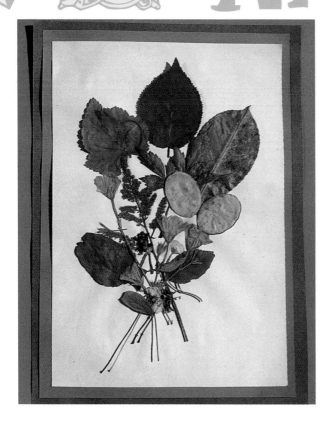

First activities

1 Dried flower pictures

These were popular in Victorian times. Here is how to make them:

1 Place flowers and leaves separately on newspaper

heavy book

2 Leave under a heavy book for several weeks

3 Carefully lay in position and glue down

2 Silhouettes

Place a child in profile between a bright light and a large sheet of white paper on a wall or easel. (Partially blacking out the room might help with this.) Draw the silhouette outline on the paper. Cut out the shape, draw around it on black paper and mount it on white paper.

child standing in profile

strong light

3 Accessories

Find out what the well-dressed man and woman wore in the decades of the Victorian era. Look especially at the hats, gloves, bags, canes, parasols, jewellery and other accessories. Fill a card 'shop window' with drawings. Look at pieces of Victorian jewellery and discuss the materials used, the styling, and who might have worn them.

Historical elements

particular periods and societies ✓
representations of the past ✓

Further activities

1 Terraced house
Shoeboxes of similar size can be made into replica terraced houses and placed on display.

2 Costume dolls
Make peg dolls in Victorian costume, as shown below. A single pipe cleaner wound around the peg will provide both arms. The clothes can then be glued on to the doll.

Resources

Flower press or newspaper and heavy books; leaves and flowers for pressing; paper doilies; sugar paper; slide projector or powerful lamp; large sheets of white paper; felt-tipped pens; colouring pencils; shoeboxes and other cartons; junk modelling materials; wooden clothes pegs; PVA glue; fabric scraps

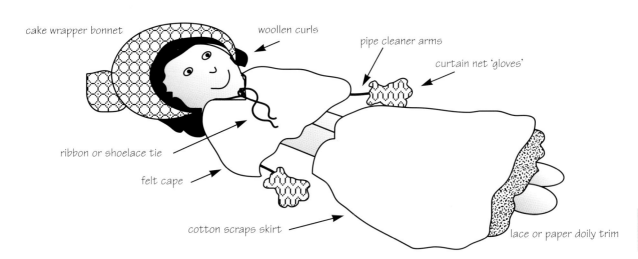

cake wrapper bonnet

woollen curls

pipe cleaner arms

curtain net 'gloves'

ribbon or shoelace tie

felt cape

cotton scraps skirt

lace or paper doily trim

Working life

First activities

1 Upstairs, downstairs

Find out about the life of a Victorian servant in a middle-class home, focusing on the parts of the house the servant could or could not enter. Ask the children to draw a cutaway picture to show the different areas of the house.

2 Patchwork

This is a traditional way of making bedcovers and other items from scraps of fabric. The patterns can be quite intricate, although the examples on page 53 include simple hexagons. If the children are not skilled enough to handle pointed needles and thread, the fabric can be stuck around the template and the card left in place.

3 My day

Ask the children to choose the role of a domestic servant or a worker in a factory in Victorian times. They should then find out what they might be doing at each hour on a typical day. The children can draw or write about the whole 24 hours, making a time chart as shown below:

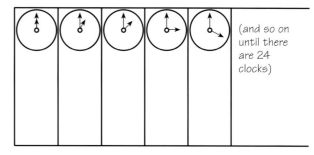

(and so on until there are 24 clocks)

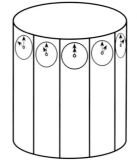

- Glue to make a continuous 'drum' showing what the worker does

Resources

Large sheets of paper; felt-tipped pens; crayons; white card; clock stamp; fabric scraps; hexagon template; card scraps; scissors; glue; needles and thread; paints and painting materials; computer software for page layouts

Further activities

1 Dressing up

Borrow stage or museum costumes of the 19th century for the children to inspect and try on. Discuss how the clothes would have felt and how they compare with the clothes young people wear today. Allow the children to draw or paint their classmates in costume.

2 Factory reform

Find out about the changes that were made in factory conditions in Britain during the 19th century. Set down the main points of each Factory Act on a scroll. Display the scrolls attached to a line across the room, linking them with drawings.

3 In the news

Obtain some copies of newspapers for dates in the 19th century. Select some news items that concern working people and enlarge them on the photocopier. Allow the children to read the items, or read them aloud. Discuss what they tell us about those times and about people's lives. Invite the children to create a news story for that time and report on it, or rewrite a story from their local paper in the style of a Victorian reporter. A newspaper page layout can be created on a computer.

Historical elements

chronology ✔
vocabulary of passing time ✔
particular periods and societies ✔
linking events/situations/changes ✔
representations of the past ✔
using sources ✔
asking/answering questions ✔
using historical terms ✔
communicating work ✔

Victorian customs

First activities

1 Rules and rhymes

Find out about some of the rhymes and expressions addressed to children in Victorian times. Create an annotated class book of these.

2 Visiting cards

Inspect some visiting cards from the Victorian era. Discuss why and when they were used. Ask the children to use a computer software package or small pieces of card to create their own visiting cards. These can then have attractive borders drawn in.

3 Wearing black

The fashion for wearing black emerged when Prince Albert died and Queen Victoria wore black in mourning for him. Jet was then popular for bead necklaces. Make some black beads, using strips of black paper and a knitting needle.

paper dipped in glue

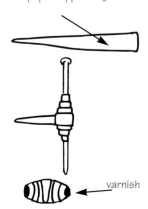

varnish

Further activities

1 Worship

The Church featured prominently in the lives of many Victorians. Take the children to visit an old local church and look for evidence of its use in Victorian times. Ask them to find some prayers and hymns written in the 19th century. Create a display of the children's findings.

purple or black drape

prayers and hymns

paper lilies

IN LOVING MEMORY

GONE BUT NOT FORGOTTEN

headstone inscriptions

2 Etiquette

As a class, find out how children and adults were expected to behave in Victorian times. For example: When should visits be made? Should children speak in the presence of their father?

3 Samplers and homilies

Make replicas of the needlework homilies that the Victorians hung on their walls. Use Binka or another kind of openwork fabric, sewing thread and blunt needles. Ask the children to mark out the stitches on squared paper before they begin stitching on the fabric. Mount the finished work in card frames.

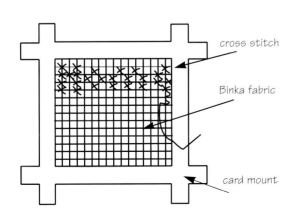

cross stitch

Binka fabric

card mount

Historical elements

particular periods and societies ✓
representations of the past ✓
asking/answering questions ✓
reasons and results ✓
communicating work ✓

Resources

Sugar paper; felt-tipped pens; computer software to create 'business cards'; black tissue paper; crêpe paper; knitting needles; paper glue; varnish; white paper; paints; Binka or other fabric with holes; thick embroidery thread; blunt needles; scissors

First activities

1 Radio and TV

Help the children to create a questionnaire that they can offer to older members of their families, asking which were their favourite radio and TV programmes. Create a class *Past Radio Times*, with pictures of personalities on the front and details of the programmes inside.

2 Travelling by train

Ask the children about their own experiences of train travel. Find out about the history of the railway, allowing the children to draw trains of various kinds. The children can look at the speeds at which trains travelled, and at the decline in the use of rail travel with the advent of the motor car.

3 Home appliances

Research the appearance, performance and ownership in Britain of a range of domestic appliances over the last five decades. Display advertisements or pictures showing these appliances in the past and more recently.

Resources

Paper; junk modelling materials; wax crayons; colouring pencils; felt-tipped pens; old catalogues of office equipment; paper glue; white card; paints and painting materials

Now

Then

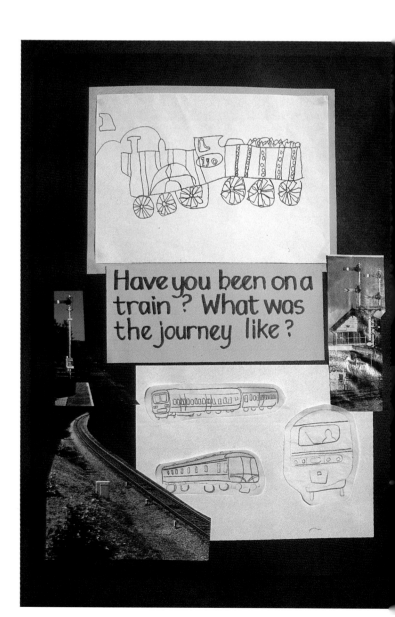

Have you been on a train? What was the journey like?

Further activities

1 Office world

Look with the children at the changes that have occurred in office life in recent times. Compare an old typewriter with the VDUs and keyboards in use nowadays. Talk about the implications of these changes for the rate at which information can be collected and sent.

2 Space travel

Explain to the children that although it is only recently that people have travelled in space, these events are recorded in history books. Obtain newspaper reports of the first moon landing, and mount and annotate them. The children can place the key events on a timeline. They can then research and draw other spacecraft that have been launched from Earth and glue these alongside the timeline in the appropriate places.

3 Environmental concern

Show the children old photographs of factory chimneys issuing smoke into the atmosphere, and talk about the changes in British law that have affected this. Then discuss current concerns about the environment, including rubbish disposal and global warming.

Historical elements

chronology ✔
vocabulary of passing time ✔
particular periods and societies ✔
linking events/situations/changes ✔
representations of the past ✔
using sources ✔
asking/answering questions ✔
communicating work ✔

World War II

First activities

1 Our families and the war

Send a letter home with the children to ask for information and photographs of what family members did in the Second World War. Collect everything together and help the children create a composite display of captions and pictures.

2 Rationing

Find out about rationing in Britain - when and why it was instigated, and what the rations for each person were for one week. Using playdough and empty food packs covered in newspaper, make replicas of the rations to put on display.

Cheese · 1 Orange · Jam · Butter · Meat · 1 Egg · Sugar · Bacon

One week's food rations for one person in Britain

3 Evacuation

Tell the children about the evacuation of women and children from cities in Britain. Discuss the experience of going away from home, and the locations to which the children were sent. Compare the things evacuees may have taken with the things children take when going away these days. Invite the children to write 'letters home', pretending that they themselves have been evacuated.

Further activities

1 How the war began

Talk about the events immediately preceding the outbreak of war in Britain and listen to Attlee's radio speech. Allow the children to copy out the speech and use it as part of a display with pictures of people in the British forces, official documents and symbols of war.

2 What women did in the war

Women's contribution to the war effort in Britain included taking on work traditionally seen as the work of men. Ask the children to find out about the jobs women did and then paint or draw pictures of them at work. Display these around a picture of a giant Union Jack flag (or use a fabric flag for the display).

Resources

Junk modelling materials; paper glue; playdough; paints and painting materials

Historical elements

chronology ✓
vocabulary of passing time ✓
particular periods and societies ✓
linking events/situations/changes ✓
representations of the past ✓
using sources ✓
asking/answering questions ✓
reasons and results ✓
using historical terms ✓
communicating work ✓

3 Local effects of the war

Consult local records and local history experts to find out how the Second World War affected buildings and the community locally. Using archive material, help the children copy and re-create evidence of the effects of war. This will focus their thinking on the changes the war brought about.

Postwar Britain

First activities

1 Change in my family

As an example of some of the changes that have taken place in family life since the Second World War (including more women working outside the home), the children should try to chronicle their own family changes, drawing pictures to illustrate these.

2 Air travel

It is only in recent times that affluence and reduced air fares have allowed many people to travel further to visit relatives and take holidays. The children could obtain data about the increases in Britain in the number of air travellers, airlines, airport take-offs, etc. and create a 'flight data' display.

3 Home improvement

Increasing automation has meant that homes can now have features such as central heating (automatically controlled), security alarms and lighting systems working on sensors, portable telephones and waste disposal units. Talk about the changes that have occurred in the children's family homes. Using an empty food box, allow the children to make a small two-part model, showing an area of a house in about 1950 and the same room now.

Historical elements

chronology ✔
vocabulary of passing time ✔
particular periods and societies ✔
linking events/situations/changes ✔
representations of the past ✔
using sources ✔
asking/answering questions ✔
reasons and results ✔
using historical terms ✔
communicating work ✔

Further activities

1 Events since the war

Examine with the children some particular events in Britain since the Second World War. The choice may be influenced by local events and the sources available. Alternatively, the children could look at the 1951 Festival of Britain. They could then compare the reasons why this was planned with the reasons why the millennium exhibition in Greenwich, London, is taking place, and make their own posters advertising the Millennium Dome.

2 What we wear

Since the end of the Second World War, 'rules' of dress have become more relaxed in Britain. Casual clothes and sportswear are worn by people of all ages. The children can look at men's, women's and children's fashions over this period, and contrast the more formal with the more casual.

Resources

A3-size paper; advertisements for airlines; travel agents' brochures; junk modelling materials; paper glue; felt-tipped pens; crayons; coloured pencils

3 Leisure

Increased 'spare' time for people in Britain has provoked the growth of the 'leisure industry'. The children can compare the choices available to British people in their leisure time 50 years ago with the choices available now. They can make a cut-out shape of someone relaxing, for each decade since the war. Information and pictures about popular music, pastimes and holidays popular in that decade can be displayed around each figure.

Fashions for women, men and children have changed in recent decades.

We wear more casual clothes nowadays.

Ancient Greek influence

First activities

1 Words we use
The children can find out some of the English words in common use that come from the Greek language such as abracadabra, politics, mathematics, orchestra and harmony. They can decorate these and pin them on a word board.

2 The work of scholars
Find out about the philosophers, mathematicians and other thinkers of Ancient Greek civilisation. These could include Hippocrates, Socrates, Plato and Ptolemy. The children can follow a 'trail' of information about each thinker, and display their findings.

3 Olympics
Seek out details of the Ancient Greek olympics, which are said to have begun as athletics contests at Olympia. Compare the details of these events with current sports. Make a model sports stadium

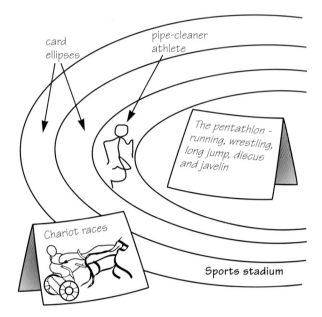

card ellipses

pipe-cleaner athlete

The pentathlon - running, wrestling, long jump, discus and javelin

Chariot races

Sports stadium

from card and tiny athletes from card or pipe-cleaners. Display details of events such as chariot races and the pentathlon along the track.

ΓΡΕΕΚ ΤΕΜΠΛΕΣ

on the modern world

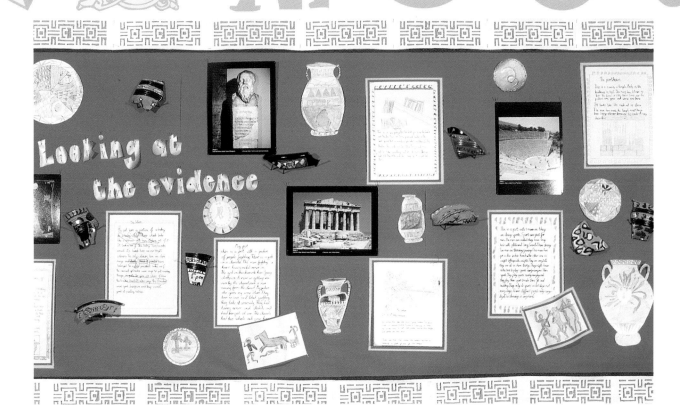

Further activities

1 Buildings and statues

The children can investigate evidence of the Ancient Greeks' building expertise. Ruins of temples and other buildings show the Greeks' use of pleasing proportions, including the Golden Ratio. (This is the ratio 1: 1.62 and can be found in many of the measurements used.) Ask the children to look carefully at pictures of Greek buildings and statues to see if they can spot this special ratio in pairs of measurements, e.g. if a statue's head is 1 cm long, then the distance from the chin to the navel should be 1.62 cm. The children can draw these buildings and statues, preserving the Golden Ratio as far as possible.

Historical elements

chronology ✓
vocabulary of passing time ✓
particular periods and societies ✓
representations of the past ✓
using sources ✓
asking/answering questions ✓
using historical terms ✓
communicating work ✓

2 Paintings

The aesthetic idea of the Golden Ratio is also evident in the shapes and sizes of paintings. Using different shapes of paper, the children can try some portraits and judge whether some shapes give a 'more pleasing' outcome than others.

Resources

Paints and painting materials; felt-tipped pens; card; rulers; scissors; white paper; stapler and staples; paper in different shapes and sizes

Ancient Greek life

First activities

1 Clothes

Both men and women in Ancient Greece wore loose tunics called *chitons* (women's tunics were longer than men's). These were fixed with a brooch at the shoulder. Make a tunic from sheeting pieces. Allow the children to make printing blocks, using wooden pieces and string. A girdle to go around the waist can also be made from plaited thick cord.

2 Pots

The Ancient Greeks made elaborately decorated pottery and the children can try making papier mâché vases, using a jamjar or flower pot as the starting shape. Alternatively, the outline shape of a vase can be drawn on white paper. A picture is then drawn on to the vase and painted with gold and silver paints. The background can be filled in with black crayon.

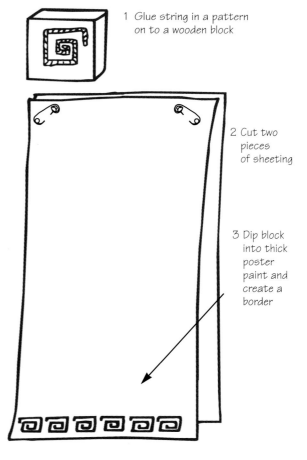

1 Glue string in a pattern on to a wooden block

2 Cut two pieces of sheeting

3 Dip block into thick poster paint and create a border

3 Eating and drinking

Ancient Greeks are often depicted lying on a couch to enjoy a meal. The children can work in groups to make couches for 'lightweight' dolls.

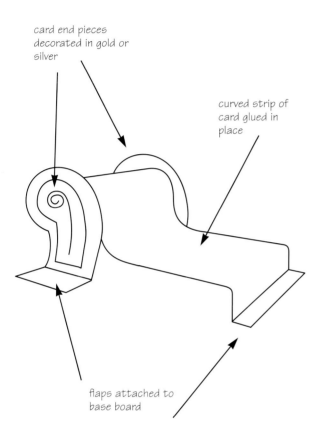

card end pieces decorated in gold or silver

curved strip of card glued in place

flaps attached to base board

Further activities

1 Gods and goddesses

List the 12 main gods and goddesses of Ancient Greece and the areas of life they looked after. Collect together a selection of different images of each one. Invite the children to create their own pictures, giving an appropriate portrayal of each god or goddess.

2 Decoration

The Ancient Greeks often created border prints on pottery and sculpture. The children can create their own from cut paper strips. These need to be folded concertina-fashion and then cut through all layers. The borders can be displayed on narrow frieze paper, or used as edging for displays.

Resources

Jamjars or similar containers; newspaper; paper glue; paints and painting materials; gold and silver paint; black crayons; cotton sheeting; large safety pins; pieces of wood; string; thick poster paint; plastic foam; polystyrene trays; PVA glue; silver foil; junk modelling materials; frieze paper; strips of paper

Historical elements

particular periods and societies ✓
using sources ✓
asking/answering questions ✓
communicating work ✓

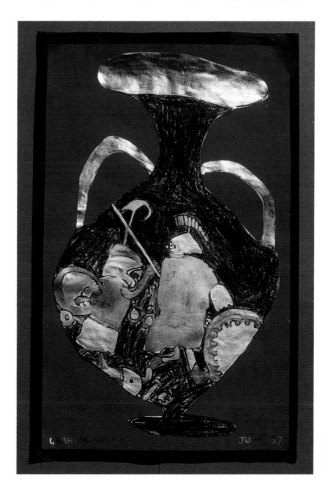

Greek myths

First activities

1 Greek legends

Many Greek myths have been retold in books for children. Read aloud some of these and find out which ones fire the children's imagination. The children can then plan their artworks.

2 Heracles (Hercules)

The children may like to paint a part of the story of how Heracles rescued Prometheus, who had been chained to a rock by Zeus, or some of the 12 labours given to Heracles by Eurystheus.

3 Theseus and the Minotaur

The children can try to paint a bull-headed monster. Using clay strips on a base board, they can also create a labyrinth in which to place a model minotaur.

Historical elements

particular periods and societies ✓
communicating work ✓

Further activities

1 Jason and the Argonauts
Create a class backdrop painting of this myth with
3-D paper embellishments of features such as the
ship's oars and the warriors' shields.

2 Medusa
The children can create clay heads of this monster
with snake-like hair who turned people to stone
when they glanced at her. Pegasus was the
winged horse who sprang forth from Medusa's
corpse. Acrylic paints can be used to create
powerful images of this creature (see page 66).

Resources

A selection of media
such as: poster
paints; watercolour
paints; acrylics; felt-
tipped pens; silver
and gold pens;
crayons; clay

Local history

First activities

1 My home

Invite the children to find out about the history of their own home. (Even recently-built houses will have a history, which may be longer than the children's lives to date.) The children can each make a book in the shape of their own house to record its history.

2 The community

Work out from local maps how the size of the community in which the school is located has changed over several centuries. As a class, create an 'artist's impression' of how it looked at three points in its history. Display these on a piece of paper, shaped to show the overall increase or decrease in size.

3 Local people

Seek out some local people who are knowledgeable about the community and are able to talk to a young audience. Allow the children to visit the places mentioned in the talk and to create a 'memory board' for each speaker.

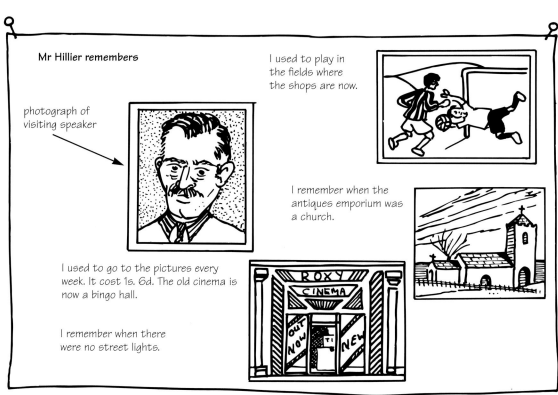

Mr Hillier remembers

photograph of visiting speaker

I used to play in the fields where the shops are now.

I remember when the antiques emporium was a church.

I used to go to the pictures every week. It cost 1s. 6d. The old cinema is now a bingo hall.

I remember when there were no street lights.

Further activities

1 Sites of importance

Find out about buildings and sites of historical and archaeological interest in the locality. Give the children access to information about them (and visit if possible). The children can then write and illustrate a guide book to their town. Groups can work on different parts of it, or each group can make the book suitable for a different audience.

2 Local heroes and heroines

List some famous and infamous people who lived locally. Working in pairs or groups, the children can research these people. Their work can be displayed under blue '... lived here' plaques on a display board. The plaques are flaps that the children lift up to read about these people.

3 'Time team'

Ask the children to make an audio tape or contribute to a video presentation about a local historical site. This can involve drawings of how things looked in the past, as well as factual commentary and role-play of incidents and conversations from the past.

Historical elements

chronology ✓
vocabulary of passing time ✓
particular periods and societies ✓
linking events/situations/changes ✓
representations of the past ✓
using sources ✓
asking/answering questions ✓
reasons and results ✓
using historical terms ✓
communicating work ✓

Resources

Paper; coloured pencils; staples and stapler; large display board; coloured card pieces; paper strips; large sheets of paper; scissors; paint and painting materials; large card circles; access to tapes, tape recorder and/or video recorder

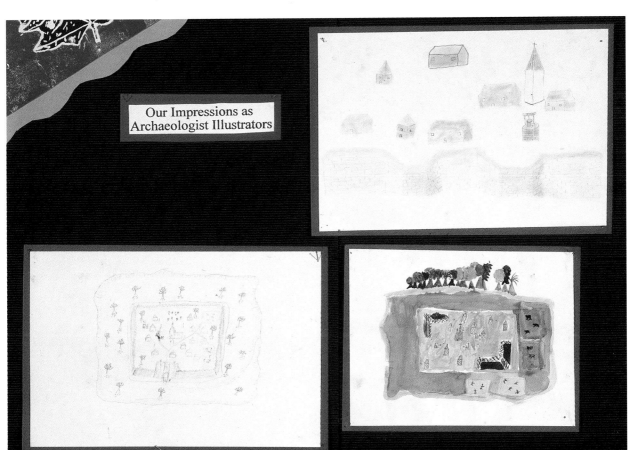

Our Impressions as Archaeologist Illustrators

Ancient Egypt

First activities

1 How long ago?
The Ancient Egyptian civilisation is said to have lasted longer than any other, so it is interesting for children to place it in time. Help the children create small booklets setting events in the past. Put a different heading on each page: 'Five years ago'; '50 years ago'; '500 years ago'; '5,000 years ago' (at the beginning of the Ancient Egyptian civilisation). The children can draw an event on each page.

2 Everyday life

Research aspects of life for the Ancient Egyptians. Allow the children to create glove-puppet Egyptians that they can use to act out everyday events such as visiting the temple, working as a slave, or farming.

3 Face painting
Look at pictures of the ways in which Ancient Egyptians made up their face. With extra adult help, use face paints to create these effects on the children. Allow the children to make portraits of one another.

Historical elements

chronology ✔
vocabulary of passing time ✔
particular periods and societies ✔
representations of the past ✔
using sources ✔
asking/answering questions ✔
using historical terms ✔
communicating work ✔

Resources

Paper; staples and stapler; felt-tipped pens; pencils; Plasticine; paper strips; glue; paints and painting materials; fabric for puppet costumes; needles and thread; face paints; plastic bottles; dolls; sheeting; acrylic paints; gold paint; white card; sand; clay

Further activities

1 Mummies

Find out how the Ancient Egyptians viewed death and how they treated their dead. Create 'mummy' dolls to add to a display of the children's writing.

2 Hieroglyphs

Look at some Ancient Egyptian hieroglyphs and their translation. Create some symbols and try 'picture' writing.

3 Pyramids

Discuss how the pyramids were built. Find data about their size. Make a scale model of some pyramids from card. Cover the card with glue and sprinkle on sand. Add people made from clay to the same scale.

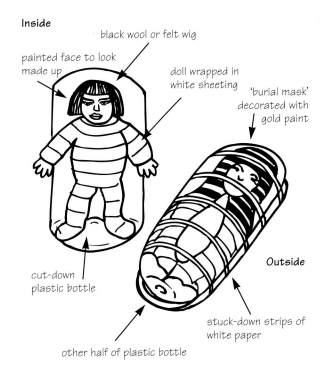

Inside

black wool or felt wig

painted face to look made up

doll wrapped in white sheeting

'burial mask' decorated with gold paint

cut-down plastic bottle

Outside

stuck-down strips of white paper

other half of plastic bottle

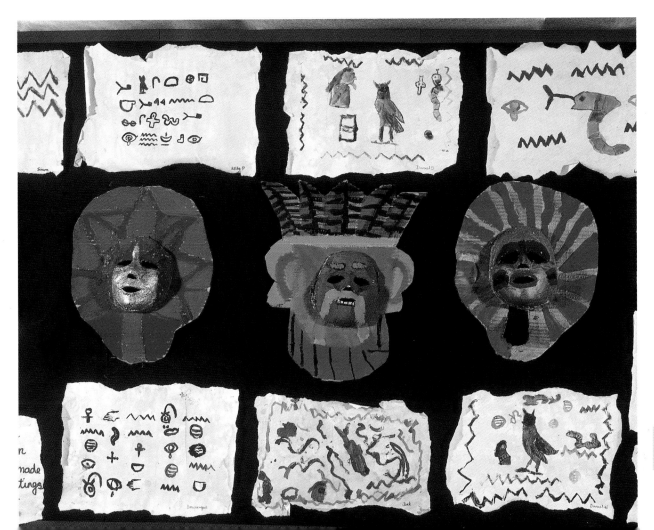

Life in the past

First activities

1 Where in the world?

Use a large-scale world map and ask the children to colour in the locations of some early civilisations such as the Benin of Nigeria and the Aztecs of middle America. Discuss the fact that many of these civilisations did not coexist, and compare the epochs for each one.

2 Decoration

Look at the decorative devices used by one of these civilisations. Some created jewellery. The people of the Indus valley made animal pictures on stone seals. The Aztecs used the feathers of brightly coloured birds to make headdresses. Some cultures also had elaborate ways of dressing their hair, e.g. the Benin, and these could be replicated in clay.

Historical elements

chronology ✔
vocabulary of passing time ✔
particular periods and societies ✔
representations of the past ✔
using sources ✔
asking/answering questions ✔
using historical terms ✔
communicating work ✔

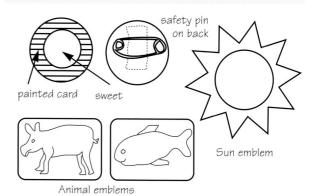

painted card   sweet

safety pin on back

Sun emblem

Animal emblems

3 Palaces

Show the children pictures of the palaces built by one of these peoples. Many civilisations designed their buildings to have tiers of floors that became progressively smaller as they went higher. This idea can be replicated with paper cylinders and card for floors and walls.

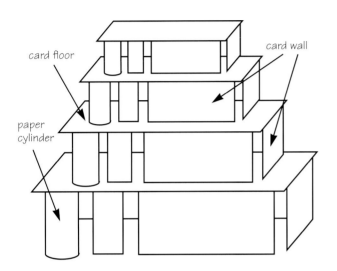

card floor

card wall

paper cylinder

Further activities

1 Treasures found

Look with the children at pictures of ancient finds. These can include figurines and weapons. Allow the children time to copy the items, noting how and when they were made.

2 Exchange

Find out about the exchange/money systems used by these peoples. (For example, the Maya used shells.) Create a game of exchange and barter in class, using found objects such as fir cones.

3 Good ideas

Assess some of the ideas coming from a study of these civilisations. For example, cleanliness was important to the people of the Indus valley, and it is said they created water supply and drainage systems. The children can draw and label the ideas for a class display.

Resources

Felt-tipped pens; clay; PVA glue; clay working tools; paper; world map; scissors; card; tape; safety pins; fir cones and other natural items

Strategies and skills

Here is a checklist of experiences that will help the children to develop strategies for historical enquiry and to acquire the necessary skills:

- Observe and handle artefacts
- Visit sites of archaeological interest
- Visit museums
- Make a replica
- Write an account (report)
- Write an account (as one of the people involved in the historical events)
- Analyse past events and express opinions
- Role-play an historical character
- Watch films made of stories from the past
- Watch factual TV programmes about the past
- Respond to a display
- Create a display
- Record people's opinions and information about the past on tape and play it back to classmates
- Enact a scene from the past in costume and record it on videotape

- Write a letter to someone in the past, asking key questions or offering advice
- Do a survey among family members about the past
- Listen to what someone from outside Europe says about the history of their nation
- Collect newspaper reports of a set of local events. Write up an 'historical' record. Add it to the school archive so that subsequent children can use it.
- Create a time capsule to be buried in the school grounds
- Look at a portrait and use clues to write about the personality and lifestyle of the person depicted
- Make a diary of an historical event
- Use historical information to make drawings of how things looked in the past
- Compile quiz questions for classmates
- Design and plan an exhibition
- Consult archive documents, e.g. parish register, school log
- Access information on CD-ROM
- Use computer software to create a record of work in history